Stand Up for Sportsmanship

Growing Character

By Frank Murphy

21st Century Junior Library

E
175 murr

CHERRY LAKE
Publishing

Published in the United States of America by
Cherry Lake Publishing
Ann Arbor, Michigan
www.cherrylakepublishing.com

Reading Adviser: Marla Conn, MS, Ed., Literacy specialist, Read-Ability, Inc.

Photo Credits: ©Cynthia Farmer/Shutterstock, cover, 1; ©barbsimages/Shutterstock, 4; ©Jakkrit Orrasri/Shutterstock, 6; ©Glen Jones/Shutterstock, 8; ©Wang Sing/Shutterstock, 10; ©Tim Scott/Shutterstock, 12; ©matimix/Shutterstock, 14; ©Dragon Images/Shutterstock, 16; ©wavebreakmedia/Shutterstock, 18; ©Rawpixel.com/Shutterstock, 20

Library of Congress Cataloging-in-Publication Data

Names: Murphy, Frank, 1966- author.
Title: Stand up for sportsmanship / written by Frank Murphy.
Description: Ann Arbor, Michigan : Cherry Lake Publishing, 2019. | Series:
    Growing character | Includes bibliographical references and index. |
    Audience: K to grade 3.
Identifiers: LCCN 2019007444 | ISBN 9781534147461 (hardcover) | ISBN
    9781534148895 (pdf) | ISBN 9781534150324 (pbk.) | ISBN 9781534151758
    (hosted ebook)
Subjects: LCSH: Sportsmanship—Juvenile literature. | Conduct of
    life—Juvenile literature.
Classification: LCC GV706.3 .M87 2019 | DDC 175—dc23
LC record available at https://lccn.loc.gov/2019007444

Cherry Lake Publishing would like to acknowledge the work of The Partnership for 21st Century Skills.
Please visit *www.p21.org* for more information.

Printed in the United States of America
Corporate Graphics

CONTENTS

You should always show good sportsmanship when playing a sport or game.

What Is Sportsmanship?

Haley was playing soccer on the opposite team as her best friend, Emily. The game went into a shootout. Haley blasted a powerful kick. The ball bounced off the goalpost. Then Emily took her shot. It zoomed right past the goalie into the net. Emily's team won.

"Wow! Great shot!" Haley said. She high-fived Emily.

Show good sportsmanship by respecting the other team
when you play sports.

Sportsmanship means treating yourself, your teammates, and your **opponents** with **respect**. It is the "golden rule" in sports. Haley respects herself by playing by the rules and giving her best effort. She respects her teammates by passing the ball and not blaming others. She respects her opponents by **congratulating** them if they win.

If everyone takes turns on the playground, everyone can have fun.

Being a Good Sport

You can be a good sport throughout your day. It is easy to be a good sport at recess. Finnegan includes everyone when playing football. He lets others have a turn to be quarterback. He **encourages** his teammates, even after they make mistakes.

Don't forget to pass the ball when you are playing basketball.

You can be a good sport on the basketball court, too. Finnegan listens to his coach all the time. He doesn't argue with **referees**, even when they call a foul on him. Finnegan passes the ball. He doesn't shoot every time he touches the ball. Finnegan gives it his all, whether he is winning or losing.

Look!

Watch for examples of good sportsmanship on the playground. Do you notice kids waiting their turn? Do you see kids sharing a ball or including other kids? What other examples of good sportsmanship do you notice?

Listening to referees is an important part of good sportsmanship.

A person who is a good sport understands that winning isn't everything. The most important thing is giving your best effort and having fun. A good sport has a GREAT **attitude**, win or lose. And remember, you can learn more from losing than from winning.

Ask Questions!

If you aren't sure about the rules of a game or sport, ask your coach or teacher. They will be happy to explain the rules. Coaches and teachers love to help kids learn how to play better.

If you don't use good sportsmanship, your coach may
have you sit out games.

What happens when you do not show good sportsmanship? Your friends might not want to play with you. Your teammates won't have fun in games. And your coach won't want to have you on the team!

How is your family like a team?

What does sportsmanship look like at home? Your family is like your team. Cheyanne **cooperates** with her family at home. She helps set the table after her aunt cooks dinner. She cleans off the table after dinner. Cheyanne's cousin helps her practice multiplication facts. They all work together to enjoy their time together.

Make a Guess!

What would happen if no one played a game by the rules? How would anyone know who is winning or losing? Think about why rules are so important.

Congratulate your friends, classmates, and teammates
when they do a good job.

Sportsmanship can be displayed in school, too. You can help a friend pick up their colored pencils off the floor. Be a team player during group work by listening to other members' ideas. Show **gratitude** to the people who help you succeed in class, whether it's a classmate or a teacher. Everyone in your class is on the same team.

If you are a good sport, you are sure to have a great time!

People will enjoy your company when you show sportsmanship. They will want to play, to work, and be friends with you. You may even **inspire** others to show good sportsmanship, too!

GLOSSARY

attitude (AT-ih-tood) a manner of acting, feeling, or thinking

congratulating (kuhn-GRAJ-uh-lay-ting) offering good wishes to someone when something good has happened to them

cooperates (koh-AH-puh-rates) works or acts together

encourages (en-KUR-ij-iz) gives support or confidence to someone

gratitude (GRAT-ih-tood) being thankful

inspire (in-SPIRE) to move someone to act or create something

opponents (uh-POH-nuhnts) the people or teams you play against in sports

referees (ref-uh-REEZ) people who oversee a game and make sure the rules are followed

respect (rih-SPEKT) a sense of caring for someone else's worth

FIND OUT MORE

BOOKS

Adler, David A. *Don't Throw It to Mo!* New York, NY: Penguin Young Readers, 2015.

Binkow, Howard. *Howard B. Wigglebottom Learns About Sportsmanship: Winning Isn't Everything*. Sarasota, FL: Thunderbolt Publishing, 2011.

Sileo, Frank J. *Sally Sore Loser: A Story About Winning and Losing*. Washington, DC: Magination Press, 2013.

WEBSITES

KidsHealth—How to Be a Good Sport
http://kidshealth.org/kid/feeling/emotion/good_sport.html
Read tips for losing gracefully and playing your best.

KidsHealth—Kids Talk About: Coaches
http://kidshealth.org/kid/talk/kidssay/comments_coaches.html
Find out what kids have to say about coaches.

INDEX

ABOUT THE AUTHOR

Frank Murphy has written several books for young readers. They are about famous people, historical events, and leadership. He was born in California but now lives in Pennsylvania with his family. Frank's friend Colin McCarthy helped write this book. Colin, an expert on sportsmanship, is a basketball coach, teacher, and former college basketball player.